Intentional Teaming

Shifting Organizational Culture

Here is to customizing supports one person at a time!

Cheers

When we connect with one another, our true human capacity emerges!

Beth Gallagher

&

Kirk Hinkleman

INCLUSION

Library and Archives Canada Cataloguing in Publication

Gallagher, Beth
    Intentional teaming : shifting organizational culture / Beth Gallagher & Kirk Hinkleman.

Includes bibliographical references.
ISBN 978-1-895418-91-0

    1. People with disabilities--Employment. 2. Corporate culture. 3. Teams in the workplace. I. Hinkleman, Kirk II. Title.

HD7255.G34 2012   658.30087   C2012-901445-1

Book cover design: Joshua Bellfy

Published by Inclusion Press
Copyright © 2012 Inclusion Press

Printed in Canada by Couto Printing & Publishing
Printed on stock containing post consumer recycled content

INCLUSION PRESS

47 Indian Trail   tel. 416.658.5363   inclusionpress@inclusion.com
Toronto, ON M6R 1Z8   fax. 416.658.5067   inclusion.com

inclusion.com   BOOKS • WORKSHOPS • MEDIA • RESOURCES

Table of Contents

For Carolyn and Jody

Preface

Kirk and Beth

Welcome to Intentional Teaming. Intentional Teaming, you ask? You are probably wondering what that means.

At its core, Intentional Teaming is the mindful practice of building sustainable support systems through fostering values-based partnerships.

We are Beth Gallagher and Kirk Hinkleman and we are, in fact, a team. As a team, we are constantly learning how to join our gifts in a way that is most efficient and most productive. The work we do to support people with developmental disabilities requires the best of us at all times. We are mindful about every aspect of a team, from the inception to the daily functioning. We examine what works as well as, and perhaps even more deliberately, what doesn't work and we don't identify a conclusion of a team because, in this work, a team is never done. A team is ever-changing and developing. Teams are in a constant state of challenge and pursuit of what comes next, all based on the person with the developmental disability and the interdependence of the team members.

Beth has worked to support people who are labeled with challenges associated with disability since 1986. During that time, she has worked to create customized supports for persons who are marginalized because of behavioral issues or other complications that have excluded them from traditional services.

Kirk has worked to support people who are labeled with differences associated with disability since 1998. For the first half of that time, Kirk worked primarily with transition-aged youth, 18 to 22 years of age, supporting students transitioning out of the school system and into living their lives as adults in the community. During that time, Kirk realized his efforts would be best used advocating and supporting adults to live fully inclusive, self-determined lives.

We feel passionately about these issues. And we trust that since you are reading this book, you want to approach the support of people with developmental disabilities in new, thoughtful and vibrant ways. Maybe you are someone new to issues around inclusion and disability, or you may already be a veteran of services who wants rejuvenation, a fresh look at how and why you can offer a new way of doing things. Perhaps you work within a corporation that is struggling with hierarchical issues. Whatever your circumstances, we hope you will be excited by the potential of Intentional Teaming to assist with team facilitation.

We have an agency in San Diego, Life Works, which provides customized support services for individuals with developmental disabilities in a variety of settings. We support individuals to live fully included lives in the community of their choice. This could mean supporting a woman who has cerebral palsy to live in her own apartment in the city, near a bus line so that she can access the local library where she volunteers three days per week. It could also mean providing support to a man with the label of autism to attend college classes during the week with a person supporting him to communicate with professors and classmates. It may take the form of providing intermittent support for a man with cognitive delays and paranoid schizophrenia as he navigates his life at work and in the community and only needs someone to help ground him when he is in a mental health crisis.

The supports we provide are varied, diverse and different for each and every person with whom we partner. People do not come in neat packages; rather, they are all fluid and changing individuals. People who have accessed services from our agency have decided to live self-determined lives instead of settling for prefabricated support systems. They want custom-built lives. We help to build a vision of the future with people one individual at a time.

With nearly forty combined years of experience working in human services as well as building and developing teams, we consider this book a narrative of our history. While this is a synopsis of what we live, breathe and believe, we recognize that there are as many theories related to support systems as there are theorists. We want to share our philosophy because it seems to be successful for all of the stakeholders involved. It isn't perfect and it will always be a work in progress, but we hope to help you prevent the "recreating the wheel" syndrome. Indeed this is a book that we wish we had access to years ago.

In the following pages, we will share how we make this work. We believe in people. We recognize that people who come to Life Works for services deserve respect and true partnership. Concurrently, we feel that the people who work with us deserve exactly the same thing. "Quality of life" is not just an ideal attached to the people receiving services.

This is also true of the teams we build. While embracing the idea of building teams, there exists a cohesive mission: to work ourselves out of a job. Our goal is always to support people to be as interdependent as possible. If we are truly building sustainable communities for people, we will no longer be a necessary support system, at least in the same manner. As that sustainable community becomes stronger, our involvement as an agency fades out of the individual's life and is replaced by natural and unpaid supports. We know some people may roll their eyes at this last statement.

However, we believe that *every* person can live successfully in the community. The challenge isn't in teaching skill sets and preparing people to be 'ready' for living a rich life, but rather it is in creating natural, intentionally built supports around people so they can live in a way that makes sense for them.

It is important to understand that the natural/unpaid resources and relationships that are built become a part of the intentional team. If everyone on the team has this common thread embedded in their daily work, then a natural cohesiveness exists. This creates the glue that holds it all together.

One reason it may seem daunting to do things in this manner is that change is difficult. It is scary to change what you already know, but if you search within, what you already know may *not* be the mission you envisioned when you got into this work. Don't let systems, procedures, practices and infrastructure, or should we say "work", get in the way of your true work. Your *work,* as defined by your belief system or what compelled you to this field, is what your everyday work should feel like. Then you are truly *feeling* your job instead of just *doing* your job.

If people are allowed to feel their work, rather than just do their work, it creates a momentum that sustains itself. However, if they are controlled to the point of simply "doing," the mission becomes stagnant. When there is no room or space set up for challenging people or letting people explore their own creativity, then the momentum won't happen. Allowing people to *own* their jobs by pursuing what makes sense to them, while being challenged to be creative, provides an environment and culture of worth.

Are you with us so far? Are you willing to explore a different way, a more interdependent way to support people to discover, nurture and realize a vibrant and fully participatory life in the community? We want to help people engage in exciting and enriching ways that benefit not only that individual, but every member of the intentional team, and the community itself. The journey is different for every person we support so what we do is always dynamic, creative and challenging.

If that sounds good to you, then come with us.

Beth and Kirk

May 2012
San Diego, CA

1

Why Teams?

Beth's Journey

For over 20 years, I worked for a wonderful company, believing wholeheartedly that I was providing cutting edge support and dynamic management and oversight. Our agency provided support services for persons with developmental disabilities, both children and adults. I was involved in everything from hiring to training to home maintenance to writing plans to intake to assessment to fundraising to whatever else needed to be done.

From my perspective, everything on my list was handled, checked off and completed the 'right' way. In the eyes of our funding source, families and licensing, I was competent and made things happen. The hierarchical culture I created was developed over many years. Out of pure ignorance, I allowed myself to believe that the way I set things up was working. That is to say, I was at the top and controlling every move that was made by people working for me. I hired and created a roster of staff who all held different job titles and duties. These people were wonderful, thoughtful, intelligent and productive employees.

The key ingredient that I didn't pay attention to was the quality of life for the people providing the supports. I felt that I was aware of the quality of life that each person receiving supports enjoyed. People's lives were good; however, it was clear that I was not mindful of creativity or the wholeness that could have been present. I was not paying attention to the amazing talents that these individuals could bring to the table.

It never dawned on me that people didn't love their jobs, or that the people's lives weren't as full and rich as they could have been. I created a self-fulfilling prophecy: I was the cog that kept that entire machine running. It seemed as though my presence was necessary for the operations to flow. This was not my intention and was not done in a conscious effort to dominate. It didn't become apparent to me until I left that this culture had been created. It was only when I was exposed to new ideas that I realized what I had inadvertently created. I was humbled.

I now sit on the board of directors of that same agency as an integral part of helping them reassemble the pieces of a system that crumbled because I wasn't intentional about developing sustainable teams.

Beth

What grounds us in our work now at Life Works is that we try hard to learn from our mistakes. Beth's experience at the agency she previously worked at allowed her to grow the concept of creating teams. At the inception of Life Works, Beth acknowledged that she needed a culture of teams and that she was part of the team, not just an administrator.

All too often there exists a dynamic wherein the person who holds the mission is promoted up the ladder to a place where they can no longer touch people. This is how the mission or the vision becomes diluted. There are layers upon layers of hierarchy between the visionary and the services being provided.

This type of situation is tragic for everyone involved. That is why there was a foundational decision made that there will never be a time at Life Works when an employee isn't a part of a team. Even as you read this book, realize team partners Beth and Kirk collaborate to bring to life our beliefs about intentional teaming. A book about teaming couldn't possibly be written by one person, now could it?

What is a team?

The definition of team is: a number of persons associated together in work or activity; to put together in a coordinated ensemble. A *coordinated ensemble* – what a poetic thought. That is what we are now. We use the concept of *team* for a number of reasons, but as in all aspects of our work in inclusion, language is the key. Everything we do must begin with the language we use. We set a tone of camaraderie by identifying our members as support teams, not as employees, staff or caretakers.

A case in point, Phil Jackson has coached his basketball teams to eleven NBA championships. From season to season, he has been able to grasp the culture of each individual team, harness the challenging personalities, guide the talents presented by each player, all while engaging every individual in the concept of 'team'. He gets his players to understand their roles on the team, and supports and celebrates each team member's gifts as a means of accomplishing the desired outcome: a championship. What we do is clearly different than basketball. However, the concept of 'team' and its intricacies are consistent across fields.

The core of a team is to be mindful of what is valued by the whole. What is the team's purpose? Once identified, that purpose must be embraced, committed to and celebrated by all people on the team; this is what drives the mission. As it pertains to working with the people we support, the mission is clear: we are trying to root people in their communities. We foster sustainable relationships, which in turn foster sustainable communities for all people.

Sustainability

Making a commitment to create sustainable teams offers relief in situations that could otherwise be catastrophic. When Beth left her previous agency, systems had to change abruptly because they were not designed to sustain themselves. Here is an example of a team designed for sustainability.

Tami & Team Tami

Tami is a woman whom we support in San Diego. She requires extensive round-the-clock support in order for her life to run smoothly and successfully. She has been in supported living for approximately three years.

When she came to Life Works for services, she decided to hire a woman named Rose, someone she had known for many years from her work program. Rose came on the team with the intention of "putting herself out of work" in regard to Tami. Rose worked the afternoon shift from 2 – 10 p.m., Monday through Friday. This was a crucial period of time for

Tami; all of her social events happened then, and it was also the longest shift when Tami was awake.

Tami and Rose were very close. During the first couple of years, Tami was terrified to have a new team member. She would become very anxious if Rose took a vacation and was extremely dependent on her. After three years Rose decided to go back to school and therefore leave Tami's team. Because Rose focused her time on helping Tami create friends and relationships with other people in her community, the transition of Rose leaving the team was seamless.

Rose saw her role as a community connector, and she helped Tami grow in confidence about her relationships. Rose was seen and valued as one member of Tami's team, one built intentionally around Tami. This was a team that not only knew each other, but that relied on each other's gifts for the success of Team Tami. In time Tami was able to rely on other people and embrace meeting a new team member. A crisis was avoided because the team members knew their purpose and worked hard to help Tami feel secure and safe.

Tami

During a Life Works hiring process, individuals are recruited to join a particular team, not merely be added to a staff roster. We aren't hiring staff and then plugging them into agency vacancies. Rather, we hire specifically for and with the person receiving supports.

When Rose left Tami's team, we didn't just fill the hole she left behind; a specific job posting was created by Tami to find a new team member. Life Works interviewed the potential team members, followed by an interview by Tami herself. Everything was done intentionally, every step of the way.

The Role of a Team Member

Now it's time to talk about the body of the team. Every team member must know what his or her particular role is on that particular team. What is it that they are intended to accomplish by being on this team?

The first thing to absorb is that the captain of the team is the person receiving services. That is the hub, the engine, the driving force behind why the team exists in the first place. Because teams are made up of diverse and unique individuals, the roles are ever-changing. As the members of the team change, so do the roles.

How are roles identified? First and foremost the needs of the captain are determined through Intensive Discovery (see Chapter 4). When those are clear, the team can create systems and plans that will address those needs and determine the actions that each person will deliver. The key is that each member knows and understands the actions of the others.

Roles can be assigned based on the gifts and talents of the individuals present. If the captain presents a need that one team member may not be comfortable with or good at, then another team member can take on that task. With this culture the indelible impression of team is created: "You have my back and I have yours." Teams are designed so members back each other up and work towards the same outcome, which is a life worth living for the team captain.

The Role of a Leader

The identification of a leader in a team is often over-emphasized. We believe that roles need to be identified. Naturally, within a team, someone will have leadership qualities. It is incumbent upon us to identify these qualities or gifts, but not elevate that person above other team members.

Due to the nature of the business, we are beholden to funding agencies and licensing and families; people have to be identified as "persons of authority or accountability." What it *doesn't* mean is that a "leader" needs to be identified within the individual teams. Having a leader just for the sake of having a leader can, in fact, erode the team. A team may have someone who has leadership qualities but rather than identifying a specific leadership role, we acknowledge and celebrate the individual's gift of leadership.

Roles naturally emerge within a team when the gifts of the team are recognized and celebrated. Leadership ability is simply seen as the gift of a certain team member, though not any more important than any other role on the team. Our societal culture is far too quick to anoint "leaders" to a deity-like level, when the truth is that leaders are simply human beings who may possess the gift of leadership. We must recognize that the gifts of the people around those leaders are different and just as valuable.

Good team builders realize that they are only as powerful as the people within the teams. Companies, unions, teams go astray when the "leader" (often self-imposed) has no connection to the team or to the effort being made to do incredible work. When all accolades are given to the Director, Manager, Owner or President, what is lost is the celebration of the journey. If team members are unhappy and dissatisfied, the quality of the work is likely to diminish. Even the most gifted team member cannot realize true potential without recognition or acknowledgment.

Recognition does not necessarily mean money, although that is always great. The power comes when people are heard and their ideas are considered and weighed evenly with those who are, by label, in the power positions. When work diminishes, the reputation of the team declines and the "leader" has less clout in the community. And when team members feel complete and are given ownership of their work, the quality and quantity both increase. You get the picture.

The creation of Intentional Teaming benefits the person being supported on many levels. It provides a framework for the team's ongoing function. The agency is positively affected as well. Intentional Teaming reduces turnover dramatically. Because team members have ownership of their job and have a voice in how things are carried out, the desire to move on is reduced. People are heard and their ideas are shared.

Each team, centered around the supported person (the captain), has a different dynamic. No two teams look the same. They are all diverse and specific to the captain, yet they all share one common thread: all team members feel supported and valued.

Creating a Job Description

This common thread of feeling supported winds its way through agency culture in some subtle and not so subtle ways. We want to dismantle the theme of hierarchy both on specific teams as well as throughout the agency. Creating job descriptions that take the person away from direct work is counterproductive.

In our case, every single person working for Life Works is directly involved in people's lives. We do this as a means of keeping each of us honest in what we do. As a result, we have job descriptions that may be a bit blurry as compared to more traditional approaches. Essentially, everybody does everything. It is our belief that persons with the label of a leader, or in our case coordinator, should not require a team member to do something that they would not be willing to do themselves.

We involve members in all aspects of the team. For example, the schedules are created and completed by the team in collaboration with the coordinator. Except in emergencies, all shift changes/coverages are taken care of by the team members in need. They are responsible for getting their shifts covered by a fellow team member. In a more traditional management style, the employee would call their supervisor and request time off. Instead, the team member is expected to communicate with a co-worker to find support in solving the problem.

This particular practice is one that we feel provides a natural shift to a joint effort in solving the problem.

Subsequently, the person being asked to cover knows that providing a little help now will more than likely come back to them when they need assistance. The idea of teaming is nurtured. The coordinator is not seen as a savior or a bad guy, merely another support. In this scenario, those whose job it is to create future plans and to design forward-moving supports are not tied up solving problems that can be solved by those intimately involved in the situation.

As noted earlier, when working with the person we support, we intend to work ourselves out of a job. Likewise, in our teams, we are repositioning ourselves out of the jobs of doing routine tasks that teams are capable of doing themselves. This creates the space and the opportunity to truly focus on the gifts and talents of the team members, and to mentor and groom people to be the leaders of the future. We don't assume that a direct support person will be in that role indefinitely; rather, we foster an atmosphere where everyone is challenged and respected. In this way more work can be done with less effort with a much richer understanding between participants. Team members learn to operate with autonomy and to understand that the confidence entrusted in them is essential for proficiency. They are addressed as intelligent, competent people and their performance, in turn, intensifies.

The Highs and Lows of Life

We afford our team members the opportunity to learn with the people they directly support through highs and lows. Team members are fully immersed in the lives of those people. It is easy to commit to someone who doesn't present any challenges or whose life is healthy and safe. It isn't easy to commit to someone whose life is chaotic. It is when a person is in distress that the true partnership emerges. When the team member is invested in the person on a deep level, then the "captain" will receive supports superior to those of a "caretaker."

John's Story

John by the pool

John is a man we have supported since early 2007. He had done irreparable damage to his vertebrae after a fall in his apartment and had been having a progressive decline in mobility for some time prior to this fall. Due to progressive cerebral palsy, aging, spinal cord weakness and arthritis, John was no longer able to walk, and instead used a scooter.

Beth met him while he was in the hospital following surgery to fuse his neck. Prior to his fall, John received minimal hours of support (twenty per month) from a wonderful agency in San Diego. On account of the lengthy recovery and the new limitations in movement, John was going to need 24/7 support upon his discharge. The former agency was not equipped to provide that type of service and so John was referred to Life Works. In February 2007, we began supporting him at home 24 hours per day.

Within a very short time following surgery, John's amazing progress took a turn. In March, after he had gone from 24/7 supports to only 8 hours per day, the surgeon found that the titanium rod in his neck had broken. This was the first in a series of relapses. He went back into surgery and the long, painful rehabilitation began all over again, but he progressed well and stayed on target for three months. He moved along so well, in fact, that he was able to get back into the pool, his most favorite place on the planet.

One day, while Beth was supporting John in the pool, she noticed that his head was tilted to one side. This concerned her. Again it was determined that the rods had broken in half. The next day John went back into surgery and had the rods replaced, and also had a halo installed. He began the excruciating rehabilitation process again that July. At the onset of this rehabilitation, he required 2:1 staffing and this continued over the next six months. Supports were reduced over time based on his physical progress.

Finally John's neck seemed to be successfully fused. We were anticipating moving forward. Then we learned that while in hospital for his last surgery he contracted MRSA (a resistant staph infection) and so had to endure months of horrible antibiotics and prolonged treatment. Again his support configuration needed to be adjusted. For the next nine months, John underwent incredible medical trauma: a bleeding ulcer, a G-Tube implantation, hospitalizations, oxygen 24 hours-a-day, a J-Tube and finally the requirement of a paid roommate to live with him.

John's medical condition has caused a great deal of upheaval in his life over the past four years. His needs have ebbed and flowed in a way that has been difficult to anticipate. While John's desire to be as independent as possible has never waned, the reality of necessary supports has stared him down again and again. The beauty that arose from the crisis in John's health is that his team stuck with him throughout. They made a commitment to John and his recovery. They were partners with him and wanted to do what it took for him to have a life worth living. Had John needed to rely only on the staffing of a skilled nursing facility in his return to full participation, he surely wouldn't have made it.

John has said over and over again that the reason he is still here is because of the dedication of his team. He needed to feel the love and to know that others were invested. He had plenty of opportunities during this time to give up, but knew that his team was rooting for him and that they had his back. John knows what commitment feels like. He knows for a fact that his team will not give in under pressure. Wouldn't it be great if everyone could know what that feels like?

This is not a new phenomenon. You have heard the expression "rise to the occasion"? You may have been in a similar situation. If you have been in a scenario where little was expected of you, your performance likely reflected that. In contrast, if you have been expected to produce, perform or act according to a higher standard, you either exceeded expectations or you tried exceedingly hard to match them.

In terms of teams of people, it is paramount to realize the intricate beauty of the individual gifts that each member possesses. These gifts comprise the essence of that team. Without knowledge of each other's gifts, there is no connection between people. The magic happens when the gifts are woven together in trust and collaboration. Without a sense of connection, we cannot partner with each other and create sustainable relationships and community.

> *"In order to build our nation we must all exceed our own expectations."*
>> Nelson Mandela,
>> Nobel Peace Prize, 1993

2

Giftedness

The Collaboration

Much of The Collaboration at Breakfast Club

Every Friday morning, our management team gathers with the management teams of two other agencies who provide similar services in San Diego. It is an informal partnering of individuals. We call this team The Collaboration, and it was born out of mutual respect, like-mindedness, and knowing the value in partnering and friendship.

Initially we came together to build strength and support amongst all three of our young agencies. We grew to understand that our real purpose was to share our gifts and talents in a way that we could not do in isolation. Each agency is stronger in advocacy and depth of commitment by virtue of being a part of The Collaboration. We call the Friday morning gatherings "The Breakfast Club".

Shafik Asante was the founder of the New African Voices Alliance and was the Director of Community Awareness Network. He used to say, "Bake it and they will come." Food brings lightness and a fusion of togetherness to a meeting. Every week a different member of The Collaboration brings the breakfast. Here again is the concept of equality within a team. These gatherings aren't director-driven and even the newest member of The Collaboration is thrown into the breakfast rotation immediately.

Here's why we feel this gathering is successful:

- No predetermined agenda

- Every member has pledged a commitment to sustaining it

- If you can't make it a particular week, there is no judgment; we'll see you next week

- It exists at the same time on the same day of the week and is ingrained on all our calendars

- There is no hierarchy

- It is casual

- There is trust

- It is confidential

- We are supportive of each other

- There is no expectation to be profound. Some Fridays we work on important and relevant issues, and others we simply sit together and gather as friends

- We are aware of each other's individual talents and struggles

The gifts that each team member in this collaboration offers are unique and valued. We know if we need guidance or support that the gifts presented by each member of this team working together will provide what we need. The Collaboration is what keeps us strong. Each individual and individual agency within The Collaboration gives and gets what they need. Everyone sees the value in it. It isn't about competition. It is about support, respect and trust. It is about being in this field together with the common goal of inclusion for all. This Collaboration is the strongest Intentional Team we have ever been involved in. The Breakfast Club is a manifestation of giftedness.

Acknowledging Gifts

> *"A gift is anything you are, have, or do, which creates an opportunity for you to interact with someone else. Under favorable circumstances such interactions can then be built into sustainable relationships and social and economic opportunities."*
>
> Judith Snow, Visionary, Consultant,
> Trainer and Artist

As an organization, acknowledging the gifts and traits people bring has a many-layered positive effect on the work being done. The team member's experience is more fulfilling and increases longevity of employment and the overall productivity of the employee. With lower turnover, the agency has reduced training costs. For the person receiving supports, it increases stability within their team.

Recognizing an individual's gifts (instead of deficits) affords that person the opportunity to contribute to their community. It provides an avenue for reciprocal relationships as that person now has a means for bartering. In our society, we often value people by what they can contribute. When we identify and value the gifts we have to offer, then we can truly feel successful.

Think about yourself and your place in your community. When gifts and talents are not clearly defined, the relationship is often take-only rather than give-take. The process of identifying these gifts can become cumbersome and we often fail to dig deeply enough. Gifts aren't always obvious.

Some gifts lie below the surface and need careful nurturing to emerge. We need to be patient and diligent in this process.

Iceberg Theory

Unless we are intentional about our relationships with people, we will never get beyond the tip of the iceberg. The Iceberg Theory pays attention to the accomplishments of people that are less easy to spot – more subtle. The obvious gifts are those that lie above the water and are easy to identify: the tip of the iceberg. What we fail to notice is that ninety percent of that iceberg lies below the surface and we don't see it unless we make an effort. Too often we celebrate the obvious gifts of people and settle at that. When someone is an exceptional artist, the gift is obvious. When an architect designs a building, the gift is there for us to see. The gift of a handyman is appreciated by his community because he has skills sought after by just about everyone.

What if your gift is more subtle? What if you are able to connect people because you require personal support to go to your corner market and grab a quart of milk? Individuals meet, and perhaps become friends, because of your need for help or because you have such an infectious smile. Perhaps your gift is the ability to demand that people slow down because it takes intense concentration to fathom your words due to your cerebral palsy.

"Among many other gifts, one of the contributions that John makes to my life is that he forces me to be still and listen, deeply. He has extremely profound conversations with me but it takes attention and patience to stay in it. My frenetic work pace and overbooked life can cause me to be all over the place. John's relationship with me does not allow for that. I am in a different space when I spend time with him."

Beth Gallagher

Because our work can get chaotic and we easily become sidetracked with the unexpected catastrophes that pop up daily, we can lose sight of our overall goal for each person, which is custom-built support. When we listen to people and connect on a deeper level, we can draw out people's gifts that might never have been discovered.

The Iceberg Theory applies equally to team members. Every person has gifts. Where we get stuck is in the discovery, in figuring out every person's less visible skills. Yes, we recognize that this person is bright, prompt, reliable, does their paperwork, is a safe driver, has CPR certification, etc. But if you delve deeper, the payoff is limitless.

Acknowledge Giftedness

Tim is a man whom we have supported for years. He is in his early forties and has a fairly serious cholesterol problem; the doctor has suggested medication. He had a team member named Angelo who had been working with him for a couple of years. As it turned out, Angelo was training to be a holistic healer. He learned of Tim's medical condition and immediately researched what he could do. He talked with Tim about some organic, natural remedies, and Tim decided to drink a daily concoction of vitamins and herbal additives including crushed avocado seed.

Within three months, Tim's cholesterol dropped 40 points. He never needed to take the medication and everyone, including his doctor, was pleased with the outcome. Traditionally, the solution would have been a pill prescribed by the doctor that Tim would be taking to this day. Our ability as a team to draw out Angelo's gift in holistic practices gave Tim an opportunity to make an informed choice. It was healthy, safe and prevented Tim from being dependent on a medication for the rest of his life.

Tim and Angelo

When people are able to explore their gifts and have them acknowledged, it builds self-confidence and productivity. By contrast, if a team member's gifts aren't acknowledged, that person becomes impotent. The team never absorbs the experiences of that person's life. It is important to remember that the members are on the team for a reason, so it would be a loss not to utilize their gifts.

> *"Every single person has capabilities, abilities and gifts. Living a good life depends on whether those capabilities can be used, abilities expressed and gifts given. If they are, the person will be valued, feel powerful and well connected to the people around them. And the community around the person will be more powerful because of the contribution the person is making."*
>
> John McKnight, Co-Director,
> Asset-Based Community Development Institute,
> Professor, Northwestern University

Identifying the gifts of each team member is crucial to a team's vitality. This should be implemented as part of the team building process. It could be as simple as just asking people what their talents are, what they have to offer the team. On many occasions people are not aware of how their personal characteristics can be seen as gifts and therefore don't share them. When helping team members discover their gifts, encourage them to share gifts that other people in their lives have found of value. You never know how a trait will become useful.

"It is Magic"

You met Tami earlier in this book. Tami has an incredible team. She has some communication challenges associated with her autism, and has difficulty saying exactly what she means. Her communication can be vague and intermittent.

Tami has many different interests and is curious to learn about new ones. She has kept a diary for years and writes in it almost daily. Historically, people have thought of her writing as a way to regulate her anxiety and have allowed her time to write. Not much attention was given to what she was writing, just that it was helpful to her.

Tami making magic

Sharmila, a woman on Tami's team, is a gifted writer. When this talent was brought out as a gift and genuine interest of Sharmila's, Tami was intrigued. As a result, Tami and Sharmila spent time together honing Tami's writing skills. Tami is now writing poetry and using writing as a more fluent way to express herself. She sends emails to Beth with descriptive language about things that she wants her to know. She is texting to initiate conversations. She is using the written word in a more consistent and deliberate way to communicate. Her needs are met much more efficiently because of her ability to write.

This has allowed a degree of freedom, independence and clarity that she did not have before. Not only that, but we have discovered some talents such as a photographic memory that could easily be the foundation for a future career. When Tami is asked about her unique talent, she says, "It is magic."

"The greatest crime you can commit is to deny someone the opportunity to give their gift."

John McKnight, Co-Director,
Asset-Based Community Development Institute,
Professor, Northwestern University

Head-Heart-Hands Tool

After spending some time understanding John McKnight's thinking about the Head, Heart and Hands framework, we created an approach to use in a team setting to help draw out hidden gifts and talents that often go unnoticed. This exercise helps people identify their own gifts.

Our Head-Heart-Hands exercise structures a process to enable people to categorize their talents and draw them out. In our template, there is a picture of a Head, a Heart and a Hand with lines below each. Gifts that we list under the Head section are those of the mind, brain, or thought, those gifts that you *know*. The Heart section is for gifts that you *feel* passionately about, that you feel connected to. The Hand section is for gifts that you can physically provide, gifts given by doing.

Keeping John McKnight's principles of Head, Heart and Hands in mind, we can use this tool to explore giftedness. Try this with a team: place a Head, Heart and Hand template on the wall for each team member present. Have individual team members fill in their own templates. When they are writing down their gifts, they need to be as specific as possible. Instead of writing that they are mechanical, they may write that they have the ability to fix foreign cars, for instance. Give them an identified period of time to fill it out (5 to 10 minutes). If they finish early, wait. Do not go on until the time passes. Let them sit in the silence.

Carolyn

Head	Heart	Hand
Music	Music	Music
Movies	Caring	Good Cook
Sports	Supportive	Home maker
Organizing	Good Listener	Community Builder
Money	Out Going	Athlete
	Kids	Organizing

Creative	Mom	Mom
Dependable	Good friend	Fun
		Dependable
Competitive	Music	Competitive Gam
Reliable	Generous	Inclusive
	Positive	
	Mom	
work ethic	friendly	playful
poetry	approachable	approachable
	invested	work ethic
	Animals	poetry
	spontaneous	
	poetry	

Try this exercise with a team:

Interval 1 – Create your poster

- Tape a Head, Heart and Hand template on the wall for each team member present.

- Have individual team members fill in their own templates. Invite them to be as specific as possible. Example: Instead of writing that they can cook, they may share that they have a favorite recipe for tandoori chicken that is really fabulous (more specific).

- Set a time limit for filling the template out, about 5 -10 minutes. If anyone finishes early, they wait in silence till the next step.

- When the time is up, ask them to stop writing and review their papers for a few moments.

Interval 2 – Read and Contribute to other's posters

- Have them travel the room and read other's posts.

- Have people write on other's templates the gifts that they see that are missing. Again, designate a period of time.

Interval 3 – Review and complete your poster

- Read your own poster noting what others have added. Add additional ideas that have been omitted.

Interval 4 – Share your Gifts of Head, Hand and Heart

- Each partner shares their poster results with the team.

Team Jamie engaged in the exercise as a team

Team Jamie reviewing what they found out about each other

When the time elapses, have them travel the room and read other's posts. Again, allow five minutes to pass. When the second period lapses then have people write on others' templates the gifts that they see that are missing. Again, designate a period of time for this activity. After that third period, let people read what others wrote and then allow them time to add things if they notice that they forgot a category. The last section is to share aloud with the group what their own templates say. In this process, new discovery may occur for each person present.

When the team is intentionally built along with the person being supported, knowing the gifts of each individual is paramount. Once this is accomplished, then the practical applications of those gifts can be woven together as a means to drive the mission of that person and his or her supports. Remember our goal: to build sustainable, inclusive communities for the people we support and to work ourselves out of a job.

3

Working Ourselves
Out of a Job

Be more poetic! If we approach things in a black and white, task-oriented mode, we may fulfill our duties, but we lose the feeling. When we are intentional about doing better work, in connecting people to each other, we are feeling the moment. If you are writing a thesis, a research paper or a newspaper article, you are using your mind. Your work consists of a compilation of facts, details and ideas. However, when you are writing a poem, you are using your whole self. You are using your heart as well as your mind. You are engaging that "feeling" aspect of yourself, which gives your mission more fuel than you had when you were simply using your mind in a purely fact-based endeavor. It provides a circumstance to be improved upon in the future, an ever-evolving continuum of change.

"If I cannot change when circumstances demand it, how can I expect others to?"

Nelson Mandela

Guess what? Circumstances now demand it. People with disabilities are demanding to be seen in a different light; to be seen, period! People are demanding inclusion. We need to change the way we go about our approach to working with people. As Nelson Mandela suggested, we need to change with the circumstances.

We invite you to entertain a different way of thinking. We can focus on data collection from countless task analysis forms documenting whether someone washes his face successfully, without any prompts, eight out of ten times; whether someone can pour a cup of juice independently five out of seven days successfully, OR, we can focus on relationships. We can document, or we can focus on relationships, all while supporting and accepting someone for who they are. When we only focus on tasks or skills of independence, we are focusing on the disability and not the person. The person becomes just another box you check off on the forms you have developed. And for what? Is the ultimate purpose to present rigorously collected and analyzed data at an IDT meeting, or is it to assist a person to live a real life?

We understand that funding requirements have to be met, and that forms exist as means of organization. So how do we keep ourselves grounded in what's important to the people we support? We prioritize *relationships* over the forms that we have to fill out. We make sure that the mandated paperwork, which doesn't have a real impact on the person's life, stays away from the person as much as possible. It simply means that we believe we should be focused on real life and real people! When we focus on relationships, we enter a world where self-worth takes precedence in a person's life.

We create a feeling of being valued by engaging people in every aspect of their surroundings. They interact with other citizens in their community in a real, visceral way as they experience real life.

The manner in which supports are designed and addressed has profound impacts on a person's quality of life. Thus, from the initiation of services, we must be mindful of how we approach support development. For too long, the human services systems have been mired in addressing skill deficits. We must ensure that a person can brush his teeth with the fewest prompts possible before his next annual review. We pay careful attention that a person can spread butter on toast without any support. If brushing teeth and buttering toast are truly the life goals of the person receiving services, then we should focus on these goals diligently. But this is unlikely to be the case. Which would you pick, developing friendships with people by hosting a game night at home complete with hors d'oeuvres and karaoke, or buttering toast? The choice is obvious. When you look at it that closely, it seems silly. We have hung onto this approach for decades because it has always been done that way. It is measurable so we measure.

Joaquin's Story

Joaquin on a visit while preparing to move to his new home

Here is an example of objectives developed for Joaquin, a man who lived in an institution until November 2011 when he moved into a home of his own. In the Discovery process for Joaquin, Life Works was developing customized supports for him to move into the community. The host of professionals supporting him at the institution called an interdisciplinary meeting to update his annual goals and objectives that would potentially be added to his Individual Program Plan. These were very well intentioned people who cared for him a great deal. On his IPP form, one goal was:

- *Joaquin will come to the medication cart the first time he is asked by 3-31-09*

Alternatively, the goal on the Individual Support Plan that his circle of support created stated:

- *Joaquin will be given opportunities to acquire a more deliberate and efficient communication system.*

For Joaquin's quality of life, which objective will have a greater impact on his happiness or his ability to engage with his community?

Elizabeth's Story

Elizabeth in her new apartment

Elizabeth is a woman we support in Chula Vista, a neighboring city to San Diego. Born with cerebral palsy, Elizabeth is one of two daughters. Her mother is Mexican and her father is Filipino. She has family spread all across Mexico and Central America, but resides in the United States for school and work. Elizabeth's first language is Spanish, but she is proficient in English. All of her education has been in the US.

For her entire life, Elizabeth's family has viewed Elizabeth as her disability and believed that, because of her cerebral palsy, she would always need to be cared for. The idea of nurturing her dreams and aspirations was never considered. Elizabeth speaks of her family as treating her like a "baby" and that it was ridiculous to think that she could live on her own.

"My family never thought that I would move to my own apartment. They always thought that I could not live independently from my mother. My grandfather opposed it the most. He would say, 'What are you going to do without the help of your mother?' He thought I was not going to be able to do anything by myself. My family would always say I could not live alone and I would say that I could with the help I need."

Elizabeth Iglesias

Elizabeth grew tired of the constant belittling of her life and decided to take action. Without any formal education on the process, Elizabeth advocated for services. She started with a friend she knew from school who was living in the community, supported by Life Works, to ask about the first step. She quickly called to set up a meeting. It was evident from the beginning that she was determined, calculated and would not accept anything less than her highest expectations for her life.

She came to the meeting equipped with the names and contact information for every single member of her team. They were friends with whom she had developed relationships through school and work. Sustainable relationships had turned into the formation of her team. Elizabeth already knew the importance of having relationships with her support team. She knew that living a self-determined life, of the quality she expected, meant that she needed people she trusted and felt comfortable with. All of her team members speak Spanish. Why wouldn't they? Elizabeth is the captain of her team. Her team members all cared about her deeply and are all on the same page. She chose not to involve any of her family who to that point in her life had been her only supports.

In San Diego, the process to receive supported living services can take anywhere from three to twelve months, but Elizabeth was tenacious and followed through. Her process was founded on the concept of having relationships with the people who would be providing her supports. This is an integral part of what we believe about intentional teams and working ourselves out of a job.

Contemplating Professional Distance

Agencies that do work similar to Life Works often embrace the idea of "professional distance." They even go as far as writing strict policies about it. In our field, many believe that when working with persons with developmental disabilities, we should never get too close or comfortable in the relationship. Life Works says it's all about relationships.

Several theories drive this philosophy. One theory suggests that if a person with a disability is learning a skill and learns it from only one person, then it becomes difficult to generalize that skill for use with others. Thus, the procedure is to change teachers on a regular basis, especially if the learner seems to be forming an attachment/connection to the teacher.

We couldn't disagree more. One of the reasons agencies create this kind of policy is for safety. Life Works inverts this belief: we say it's ALL about relationships. We understand the belief that if employees are allowed to have "friendships" with the people they support, they may be more likely to victimize them by crossing boundaries that have been blurred in the creation of that "friendship". In contrast, we believe in affording the opportunity for people to build real friendships with the people they support. And we provide training to team members on boundaries, vulnerability, power and self-advocacy, thus creating a practical awareness of safety and minimizing the risk of victimization. On the other hand, creating a policy-driven agency of professional distance creates an "us and them" atmosphere. The imposed boundaries make support impersonal.

What emotion is evoked when you see people in the community wearing a shirt that says "Staff"? The chasm that is created with a simple word on a shirt is enormous. You have set the tone of your relationship by wearing that shirt, or announcing that you are paid to be with the person. That relationship is contrived, unnatural and forced. How can we expect a true relationship to emerge under those conditions?

We both came from these molds. We know that the people who work under these circumstances are by and large good people, people who are well intentioned. They care about the people to whom they provide services. The problem is the belief framework in which we are trapped.

We started this chapter by talking about change. Now we challenge you to make a positive change in the cultural structure of the place you work. Relationships are everything. We are encouraging you to advocate for real relationships. Carefully consider the policies and procedures that are in place regarding relationships. Change the guidelines and beliefs that drive your mission. We are asking for you to entertain the idea of change. Let's not continue doing the same thing over and over because that's the way we learned to do it, and that's how it has always been done.

Kirk's Epiphany

My experience began at a residential campus for children and adults with myriad disabilities. I needed a part time gig while attending school and landed at this place. The particular dorm I worked at was for adolescent boys, ten in total. There were ten different dorms on this campus, with residents of different ages. I was assigned to be a one-on-one attendant to a boy with a diagnosis of Mild MR, ADHD and who was a sexual perpetrator, which is why he needed a one-on-one attendant. Trial by fire indeed!

I was quickly taught who he was and how he was supposed to operate or comply with his situation. We called it a 'program'. The boys would come home from school, which was also on that campus, at around 3 p.m. The first part of the 'program' was for the boys to go straight to their rooms for 30 minutes. This was supposed to ease the transition from educational program to residential program.

The next step was a pre-determined snack, placed before the boys on the dining room table. Following snack, there was the 'group meeting' in the common area or family room. Here we would let each boy express any issues he had from the day, assign staff to a few of the boys, unless someone needed a one-on-one, and let them know what we would be doing that evening.

Following the meeting, we would do an 'activity'. Half the boys would get in the van and usually drive around aimlessly through the community, strategically wasting time, while the others would go to the playground on campus, or go for a walk around campus. Dinner followed. It was sent to the dorm from the main kitchen, thus taking choice out of the equation. After dinner there was a small amount of 'free time', usually about 30 minutes, followed by 'hygiene time'. All ten boys showered at the same time, got ready for bed at the same time, and all shared the same bedtime, 9 p.m.

I forgot about the training I received prior to actually working at the dorm. I received sixteen hours of training on how to restrain people. I learned how to pivot and parry, how to do one-man, two-man and three-man takedowns. I learned how to effectively execute a basket hold. I learned that when someone gets upset, the safest thing to do is to physically intervene. This was my first foray into the field, so to me nothing seemed out of the ordinary. I actually remember being fascinated by the entire process and eager to put the techniques I had learned into practice. That changed quickly.

Then there was the other part of the 'program' that I neglected to mention: the real moments. All of that scheduled, monotonous manipulation of life that we insisted the boys adhere to created significant discord. There were constant power struggles, fights, restraints and holds. These boys were 'out of control' and our dorm had a reputation. The staff, mostly people in the same position as me, were new to the field and part-timers. We built a strong camaraderie, but burn-out was high. Shifts could span the entire spectrum of human emotion. It began to become apparent to me that what we were doing was not natural, and that it wasn't the boys who were 'out of control'. It was the system they were in that refused to recognize them as valid human beings – with valid feelings and desires. They had little to no choice over anything in their lives, and we expected them to be 'compliant' about it? It wasn't right.

My dorm was a feeder dorm to another, one operated more like a group home. Our boys could 'graduate' if they showed the ability to comply with the 'program' laid before them. Could they complete meaningless goals on an IPP? Could they get through a week without having a physical 'aggression'?

We worked under the Continuum Model, where people graduated to different levels of 'community living' based on performance. The manager of this other dorm, Jeff, would walk with his residents back from the education side of the campus, something unheard of for managers to do. Our dorm was on his way back to his dorm, and we would cross paths rather consistently. We started with small interactions that grew into longer conversations. Word around campus was that he wasn't 'appreciated' by the administration of the campus. He was a 'boat rocker' and didn't really comply with the standard way of doing things. It took me a while, but I eventually visited him and the residents at the dorm. The 'program' I listed previously? Blow that up and envision what typical teenagers would do when they got home from school. That's what they were doing. Further, the door to Jeff's office was open! The manager's door at our dorm was usually shut. The residents were free to come and go as they pleased. Where choice was lacking in our dorm, it flourished in his.

What was the problem that the upper brass was complaining about? Jeff was listening to the residents who lived at that dorm. That's it. It was a revolutionary idea for a place like this, yet such a natural aspect of life for those who live inclusively in the community. This is what everyone was so upset about? For me, professionally, Jeff was my first real mentor. He simplified what had been imbedded into my understanding of what support had to be for individuals with a label of disability. In fact, it was the genesis of the idea that disability has nothing to do with supporting people. You simply listen. Establish a relationship with the person you are supporting, treat them as you would want to be treated. It was a concept that blew everything I had learned out of the water, all the while making more sense than all of my previous training.

It was here that I affirmed that I was in the right field, that I had been doing the wrong things and that I needed to unlearn what I'd been taught. Making a connection with someone is everything. People crave it. I am forever grateful to Jeff. He provided my epiphany moment, and it has shaped who I've become today.

> *Do I regret the years I spent on that campus? No. I feel like it was vital to my evolution of mission and philosophy. Without it, I might not feel as strongly today about what I do. It is important for me to embrace that experience and use it as one of the many fuels to my fire."*
> Kirk Hinkleman

Significant Connections

We believe in building significant connections as a means to creating *new* significant connections. If we are trying to work ourselves out of a job by connecting people to others and building sustainable relationships, then don't we need to foster an atmosphere of connection to the people we provide services to? If we want to breed sustainable relationships, then we need to know the people deeply, with every ounce of who we are. We expect the people who are stakeholders in our agency to be invested in the people we provide services to. It is crucial that the entire intentional team is engaged with the person receiving supports. That person is the captain of each team for a reason and why we do what we do. Focusing on relationships rather than adhering to professional distance will keep us on the mission at hand: working ourselves out of a job.

We are not caretakers. We are people who support people to make connections. Sure, an aspect of our job may involve doing tasks that fall under health and safety or personal care, but it doesn't in any way define what we do. We are teams building community in and around the captain of each team. Caretakers work to complete a shift or a finite list of tasks. Community builders work to develop the capacity of others. That is the difference we want to emphasize.

What we are talking about is helping someone build a life worth living. People with disabilities aren't asking for atypical things. They aren't asking to live in the Taj Majal, or go to the moon. Rather, they are asking for typical lives. They are asking for relationships – meaningful, sustainable relationships. We over-complicate things in reports with unnecessary rules and meaningless goals. We get in the way of people connecting because of our own fear of the perception of our relationship to someone labeled with a disability.

Children tend to think purely about this concept. For example, two school-aged kids play together as Cory and Sam, not as Cory and the kid with a diagnosis of autism who happens to be named Sam. Cory and Sam get along great because their relationship was founded on mutual interests and meshing personalities. It wasn't based on fabricated situations. They didn't see autism as a hurdle to jump over. Cory sees Sam, not the autism.

We often get in our own way and, in turn, get in the way of allowing natural relationships to happen for people we support. Why do we interrupt natural relationships from happening? Because we have goals in a report to adhere to? Because we are anxious? Because we feel that we need to explain about 'disability' to the people who might meet this person? There are times when our arrogance gets in the way and we feel like our job requires us to set up the relationship? We need to get out of the way!

Kirk Hinkleman with "The Bee"

The Frisbee Theory

Our professionalism can sometimes create a clinical situation out of something that is as simple as an introduction. Community building is not rocket science. It does require some grace and some courage to take a risk. But it is not so complicated that it involves someone with a PhD or significant schooling in order to be successful. If you take a look around you, community building is happening everywhere. When you look even closer, the group of people that is consistently successful at this is young children. Why is this? Possibly because there are no learned behaviors around self-doubt, fear of judgment from others or socially determined boundaries. What can we learn from them? We can learn to move into someone's space just a little bit closer. We can learn that asking for what you want is not wrong. We can learn that bringing a small smile to someone's face could be the catalyst to a connection. Simply put, what we are trying to achieve is the idea of living *with* people instead of *around* them.

In July of 2011, while at the Toronto Summer Institute on Inclusion (TSI), a friend of ours, Peter Leidy, brought a Frisbee. On the second day, when Peter brought it out, we dubbed it The Bee, and began tossing The Bee all over the streets of Toronto. People involved in our gathering joined throughout the week, sometimes at the venue where we were gathered, other times whilst cruising into the city.

A couple of times The Bee flew into construction zones where we were compelled to communicate with security guards and construction workers. Another time, The

Bee landed on the streetcar tracks, destined to be crushed by the oncoming streetcar, only to be saved by the grace of the streetcar operator who stopped so we could retrieve it. The Frisbee taught us many lessons and presented us many gifts that week. In fact, a poem emerged at the end of the week, which put to words what the Frisbee had provided us to us all (see page 58).

What was born from the week was the idea, or perhaps theory, of how to approach our work: the Frisbee Theory. We began tossing The Bee to strangers, members of the Toronto community at large, going about their day unaware of our existence until the mere presence of a Frisbee acted as a bridge, a connector. People native to Toronto caught and tossed The Bee. People from Pakistan, China, Holland and Brazil caught and tossed The Bee. People with differing values, beliefs, orientations and goals all caught and tossed The Bee, all together in a moment where an opportunity to realize that we all live *with* each other became apparent. It seemed as though every time The Bee appeared, people dropped any thoughts of judgment or pretense. People began to be with each other instead of around each other.

The simplicity of the Frisbee represents where we need to get to. It acted as a common thread that week, and isn't the common thread what we seek in terms of building community? Let's embrace this idea of simplifying things to a Frisbee-like level, a level where people can Bee together. We all could use a little Frisbee Theory in our lives and it just may end up making the connections we have with our fellow community member that much more accessible, natural and sustainable.

The people we support need to build natural relationships with people in their community and lives. We need to take a different look at where and how we are spending our energy. Instead of wasting our efforts on creating policies that don't allow real relationships or interrupting the natural flow of friendship by creating contrived events, why don't we get to know the people we are supporting more deeply? Who are they? What are their likes and dislikes? What do they like to do for fun? What are their favorite foods? What are their favorite bands? What are their plans for the future? Do they want to own a house? Rent? Where do you want to live? What is important to you?

Do any of these questions have to do with disability? No. They have to do with who a person is. It's pretty difficult to help someone build a sustainable relationship with someone else if we don't know the answers to these simple questions.

Frisbee

Such a simple piece of plastic
Shouldn't mean so many things
Yet nothing short of fantastic
Such beauty with each fling

What lessons did you give this week
While you flew all over TSI
What gifts did you allow us to seek
Soaring through the Toronto night sky

When you decided to rest on the trolley car track
It appeared you were destined for deliverance
But as the trolley car stopped a bit back
The lesson emerged... tolerance

Not once, yet twice you journeyed into
construction zones
Finding yourself in need of emancipation
Through global security conversations amidst
construction worker cones
The lesson emerged... collaboration

Perhaps you were a common thread
A pure builder of community
Critical was the light that you shed
The gift emerged... unity

Your flight at times radical, other times like a dove
Tossed and caught by hands of such diversity
You have connected all of our love
And the gift emerged... a Frisbee

Kirk Hinkleman

4

Intensive Discovery

There are different ways of discovering who people are and what they want. It is called Intensive Discovery, because that is what it is: intense.

An outstanding byproduct of the discovery process is that it acts as the realization of a "voice" for the person being supported. They are actually being heard. Most often, the person receiving services has rarely, if ever, been truly heard by others. There is often a disconnect between the person's thoughts and what is interpreted by others.

We, as professionals, get a snippet of information from someone, and then turn that into a dissertation on the person's life. It's almost parental in nature. There is an assumption that we really know someone because we have done thorough assessments and read their file. We need to, as we've said time and again, get out of our own way and truly listen to the person we are discovering. How do you listen more deeply to people? Through discovery we find out what the person is interested in, what makes them tick, what are the best tools to support them and what have been the failures of the past.

Waddie Welcome & the Beloved Community

Waddie Welcome

The book "Waddie Welcome & the Beloved Community", by Tom Kohler and Susan Earl, provides an example of how an intentional team was used to afford Mr. Welcome a chance to have his voice heard. The team worked to discover who Mr. Welcome really was and what he wanted his life to be like. We recommend you get the book (www. inclusion.com), but for our purposes, here is a thumbnail summary of the story…

Mr. Welcome lived in his family's home until he was in his seventies. After his parents died, his brother took care of him, but not to the satisfaction of concerned neighbors who called Adult Protective Services. Mr. Welcome was placed in a nursing home where Tom Kohler met him and began looking for a citizen advocate, a private citizen who would become an ally and spokesperson for Mr. Welcome. Kohler is the Executive Director of Chatham Savannah Citizen Advocacy in Savannah, Georgia, a small organization with a goal to foster intentional relationships.

> *"Citizen Advocacy is built on one-to-one,*
> *freely given personal relationships between*
> *two people. One is a person with a disability*
> *who has been excluded from typical community*
> *life and the other is a person living a good,*
> *ordinary life here in our community. Friendship,*
> *spokesmanship, social support and social*
> *change can all emerge from these intentional*
> *relationships."*
> *Chatham Savannah Citizen Advocacy*

Kohler asked many people to come forward and enter into an advocacy relationship with Mr. Welcome. In fact, Mr. Kohler asked 39 people to partner with Mr. Welcome and they all said no. He kept on asking. This took time, and in that time, the state closed the nursing home and sent Mr. Welcome three hours away to another nursing home in rural Georgia. Mr. Welcome was a man with cerebral palsy who couldn't use his voice to communicate. In the book, Kohler says: "I asked if he wanted to come back to Savannah. Every muscle in his body screamed, 'Yes!'"

Positive change began when Tom Kohler discovered Addie Reeves, who he has described as a "guru in her community". At 86, she revealed that she had promised Mr. Welcome's mother on her deathbed that she would "watch out" for Mr. Welcome. She had done that for forty years.

Armed with this powerful story, Kohler continued asking until he connected with Lester Johnson who agreed to become Mr. Welcome's advocate.

Back in Savannah, Mr. Welcome became a member of a group of people called The Storytellers. Here, intentional teams of people formed support circles to help some of its members leave nursing homes. The Storytellers met monthly, ate together and shared stories and ideas. Mr. Welcome, Lester Johnson and Mrs. Reeves joined others to form a team for him. They were finally able to work together to help Mr. Welcome move into a home where he could, "smell good food cooking and hear children playing," a dream that he had shared with his team members.

Mr. Welcome's story shows one way of using the process of Intensive Discovery to understand the wishes and goals of the team captain. The support circle, or intentional team, had to think creatively to discover how to listen deeply to Mr. Welcome. Although he didn't use verbal communication, he "had a lexicon of language in his face". When presented with questions in a yes/no format, he was able to "paint a clear picture of what he wanted his life to be like". Then, roles for team members could be identified. Members knew what tasks they needed to carry out and they moved with intention, fervor and purpose. Mr. Welcome, the team captain, drove his life in the direction that he wanted. This was possible because a group of people were willing to go through the process we call Intensive Discovery.

At a reading of the book in our conference room

Mr. Waddie Welcome - living the good life...

This story gives insight into how an intentional team can begin, develop and sustain over time. If it has purpose, direction and a shared mission, it can reach its desired outcome. For Mr. Welcome, returning to his home community was the desired outcome. For our everyday work at Life Works, the desired outcome is the development of a sustainable community for all. Everyone we support has a different vision for their life, a different vision of their own personal community. It is incumbent upon us to help people realize that vision, to bring it to life.

For us, the way to start is with Intensive Discovery. Finding new ways to listen and pay attention are challenges we need to take on. Using the discovery process, we listen deeply and learn about the person's interests and feelings.

Over the course of the past couple of decades, we have spent time learning from and studying with some of the world's leaders in person centered planning. From these amazing observers of human nature we have gained insight, skillful discovery and an array of tools that allow us to be available to people in their most vulnerable moments. There are many approaches that we use to do this.

PATH

PATH is a creative planning tool which starts in the future and works backwards to an outcome of first (beginning) steps that are possible and positive. Developed by Jack Pearpoint, Marsha Forest and John O'Brien, PATH has become a tool that has profound effects on the people who use it as a means of planning for their future. (See www. inclusion.com for more information.) We have both gone through the PATH process and experienced the effect it can have both personally and professionally.

We use PATH frequently when supporting the people receiving services from our agency. It provides the foundation of the vision that each person is trying to achieve and it serves as a resource for the teams built around the people we support. We also facilitate PATHs for other interested

Elizabeth's PATH, reviewing the dream…

people. We believe in planning, and this particular tool feels as if it works very well in helping anyone who uses it to realize their purpose and how to apply it in their lives.

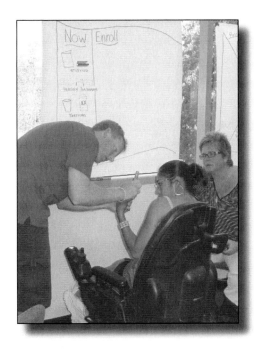

Enrolling Elizabeth, coloring her thumb for her to place her print on her PATH

Essential Lifestyle Plan

Created by Michael Smull, this plan brings a person's circle together as a way of helping others learn who a person is on a deeper level. For us, as people are referred to our agency for services, it allows us an avenue of gaining insight into a person whom we have never met as a starting point for Intensive Discovery. It provides instant momentum for us as we begin to provide supports and start to build that person's team. We spend time with the individuals who know the person receiving services very well.

Beth gathering information on a person preparing to receive support from Life Works

Our goal is to gather the information from those with the experience, the stories and the relationship. We want to avoid recreating the wheel at any expense. The end product of the Essential Lifestyle Plan (ELP) will be as close to a 'How To' book about that person that you can get, a document of clear, concise and specific information.

Liberty Plan

We developed this tool after identifying a need for something different in futures planning. We had a PATH scheduled for a man who wanted to gain some traction and direction in his life. Upon meeting with him prior to the event, we found that his anxiety over the scope of a PATH was so high that it was going to interfere with the process and his ability to follow through. However, the invitation to his PATH included people from all over the country. Cancelling the meeting was not the preferred option. In asking a few more questions, the Next Best Questions (see Chapter 5), we figured out that the open-endedness of the dream section was creating palpable angst. So the Liberty Plan emerged.

The Liberty Plan was originally designed to satisfy the planning for people that were experiencing anxiety or ambivalence around the process. While the initial use is different from graphically facilitated planning such as PATH, it is also being used successfully for teams in brainstorming sessions. Below are the steps involved:

1. Start the plan by encouraging the 'star' to share what they like about him- or herself. Always begin with the 'star', and then when those ideas are exhausted you can open it up to others if the 'star' person is comfortable with that.

2. The second section is critical in helping the 'star' person become grounded and gain confidence. This is when we spend time recognizing and celebrating accomplishments in each area of the person's life.

Liberty Plan Template

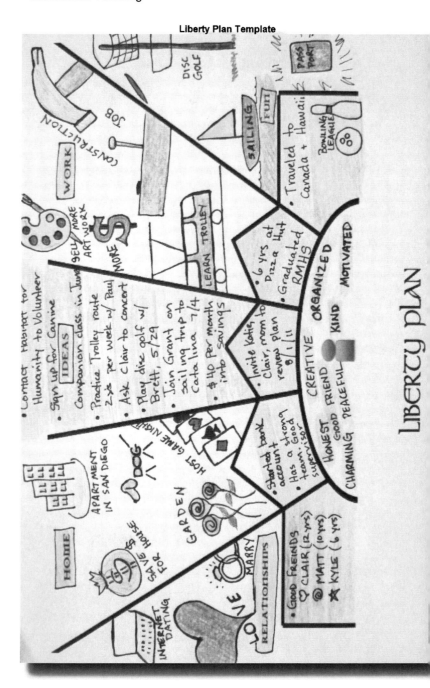

Gradually you will notice the comfort level go up and moving on to the next section is much easier.

3. This section is designed to allow people to make decisions categorically. The headings can be changed to fit the setting. You can make the theme entirely work-related or entirely home-related.

4. Be flexible. This section should be facilitated as a "regulated free-for-all". The facilitator must set ground rules in order to be able to keep peace and control within the process. It should not look chaotic, but it can be challenging.

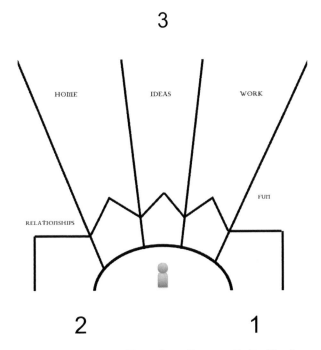

The Liberty Plan Template Connectivity Tool

Connectivity Tool

We developed this tool after identifying the importance of being effective connectors of people. What is it we truly seek? What do all human beings crave? What makes us a success in society? The answers may be different for some people, but we believe that fundamentally we all seek the same thing: connection.

A connection to oneself and to others as a means of having a true community is what lies at the core of what we strive for in our work. The word "independent" gets over used in our field. In reality, what we are actually after is "interdependence."

To be interdependent with others requires different skills. It implies sharing of responsibility. It requires you to know who you are as a person and the gifts you have to offer to others. You must feel a strong connection to yourself, and be comfortable conveying your essence to other people in your life and community. Knowing who you are and how that relates to others is vital. But even more important is the ability to see the gifts in others. When we begin a conversation with intention, with our gifts and the gifts of others in mind, we can begin to build a sustainable connection.

When connections and relationships evolve from intentional conversations, we see the development of interdependence with each other. This interdependence then begins to reach others who may not be connected, yet live in our community. As agencies, and as citizens in our communities, we must be mindful of this connectivity that

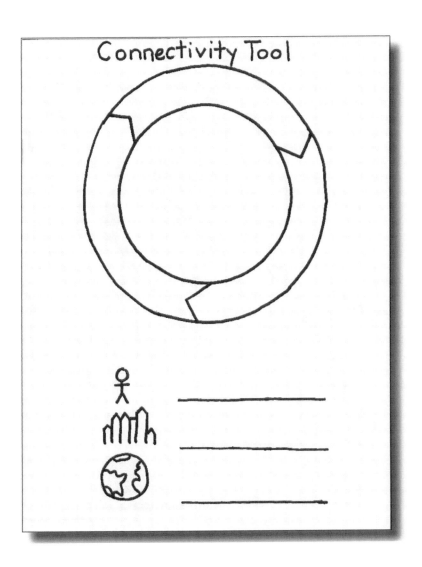

Connectivity Tool

Self: teach reciprocity

Community: create sustainability

World: embrace diversity

we all need. No one person can navigate life independently. However, if we are interdependent, we can support each other through the highs and lows of life.

Find that connection to yourself and to others, and you will experience the visceral power of community. Here are the steps in using the Connectivity Tool:

1. Provide a Connectivity Tool template to everyone participating.

2. Give people 5 minutes to think about the three values that they feel define them best.

3. After they have identified their three values, give the group 10 minutes to think of an image that represents the combination of the three values, something that will represent connection to oneself – a sort of personal logo.

4. Once the personal logo has emerged, give 15 minutes for discussion with the group about how this Connectivity pertains to connection with self, with the community, and with the world.

While specific training for tools such as PATH is encouraged and necessary, we should always use person-centered thinking. Everyone can, and should, learn more techniques, hone their skills and refresh appropriate facilitation practices.

What we don't need training on is the notion of always being in person-centered thinking mode. Even when not using a planning tool, we need to be living the philosophy of working inside out. We always keep the person receiving supports, the captain of the team, at the center of every thought and action. These tools and activities are used as a means of intentionally customizing the supports provided.

Why is it important to customize every aspect of a person's life? First of all, when we use the word 'customize', we acknowledge that everyone has a different definition of what they would like his or her life to look like. We must approach planning in that way.

Customizing is another way of saying personalizing. Our homes don't look the same as your homes. Our jobs don't look the same as your jobs. Having a place to live isn't the same as the experience of living in your own home. When you move into a house, you organize your furniture. You decorate the walls with art or paint specific colors. You make the house your 'home', which personalizes it. You buy a bedspread that typically reveals something about your personality. You fill your refrigerator with the food you love.

Similarly, having a job isn't the same as experiencing a fulfilling career. Congregating with people isn't the same as experiencing a relationship with someone. There is a tangible difference between existing in a contrived setting as compared to experiencing a visceral life.

So what leads us to a deep understanding of a person? It lies in knowing the Next Best Question, a question that will always exist.

5

The Next Best Question

Supporting people to create lives worth living is a dance of curiosity and action. We are constantly taking a snapshot of people's lives to check in with where they are. There is no time for stagnation. Status quo isn't an option unless each person individually says that they are satisfied with their life as it exists in that moment. We should constantly be in "planning mode", an ever-evolving conversation with people so that they know they are being heard and encouraged to dream. We need to keep asking the next best question.

While curiosity and planning are undeniably significant, often we find the quality and value of the planning that is being done to be substandard. How is this? How can we be working so hard doing this work and still getting it so wrong? The answer may be in our arrogance! We become numb to the distinction between the work that we are doing and the life that the person being supported is living. They are two completely different points of view. We go home at the end of our workday and carry on living our own lives. The people we support are involved in their lives continuously. When we get to the point that we no longer have the curiosity to ask questions, then we are stuck and the work becomes diluted and routine. It is the team's responsibility to keep asking questions, whether it be to solve a problem or to keep people's lives fresh.

One of the most common mistakes we make is to think we know the answer. We stop asking questions because we lead ourselves to believe that we already solved 'the problem'. It is as if we are afraid of knowing more information.

Joaquin's Story

Joaquin enjoying his evening tea

When our friend Joaquin was referred to our agency for services, we got an extensive collateral packet with all of the information about him that we would ever need to know.

It gave dissected explanations about all parts of his life from behavioral to medical to personal care to socialization. One of the topics was hygiene, so the packet answered the question, "Can Joaquin brush his teeth?" The answer was No. Typically, this would end the inquiry; the answer was clear and we slip into the assumption that we now know all we need to know, right?

Wrong! Fortunately we are intensely curious people. We figured that the person who would have the task of brushing Joaquin's teeth that very first morning of support would need to know much more than whether he can do it on his own. We began asking questions and did not stop until we had a very clear picture of possibilities. "Does Joaquin need hand over hand support?" "If you were to provide the most successful support to him, what exactly does that look like?" "Does Joaquin have any dental disease because of this issue?" "If I get close to Joaquin's mouth, what might happen?" We kept asking the Next Best Question until we arrived at alternative answers.

Joaquin is not able to brush his teeth on his own. He needs total assistance with this task, but that might look different from day to day. It might be handing him his toothbrush with toothpaste on it and guiding it to his mouth, or actual hand over hand assistance, or even at times doing it for him. He might need to move around during this process and appear to be resistive. But, we discovered that Joaquin is easily redirected if the support person allows him time to finish and is not pushy. He needs a great deal of time and a lot of space.

As we reframed this experience, we realized we could increase the probability of success by following a few emergent guidelines:

- allow Joaquin lots of time to finish successfully;

- let Joaquin know what you are doing ahead of time;

- don't move quickly or aggressively towards his face (he may feel the need to defend himself);

- use slow, deliberate movements;

- be sure to tell him what you are doing;

- don't rush...it won't work.

In this scenario we kept asking the next best questions:

"What does that situation look like?"

"If I were going to set up this task for success, how would I do that?"

"What can I do for Joaquin, to be sure he will be as successful as possible?"

"Are there parts of this task that Joaquin can do independently?"

"On the parts that he needs support with, is it hand over hand or verbal prompts or perhaps something else?"

The other questions may be:

"Does Joaquin prefer a certain type of toothpaste?"

"Would an electric toothbrush work better for him?"

We need to keep the curiosity alive. As soon as we feel we have finished asking questions or we become too lazy to ask, that is the moment when we need to stop doing this work, or seriously review our roles in it. Once again, remind yourself that this is someone's life. They can't afford for us to be uninspired about how we provide these supports or settle for "good enough".

Does this chapter speak to you? Does this book speak to you? Does it make you just a little bit uncomfortable? Does it make you significantly uncomfortable? Or is it like looking in a mirror? Does it validate what you are already doing? Then the questions might be: how can I challenge myself to be better? How do I open myself up to the discovery of something new? How do I create a situation where the 'common good' we all seek in life is at the forefront of my work?

We hope that it makes you think creatively about the supports that you are currently designing. If we have done our work, it will get you a little unsettled because consistently being a bit unsettled seems to be the most effective place to act from – not completely comfortable and not awkwardly out of sorts, just alert, curious and unwilling to be complacent.

We leave you with Tim's story, a story that presents all the elements we discussed throughout the book. Intentional Teaming was born from our experience and passion. We encourage you to read this last story and then ask yourself… what is your Next Best Question?

Tim's Story of Intentional Teaming

Tim is a man who lived in a group home from age three to 33. To most people, including Tim, it seemed that he was leading a good life. He had a place he called home and foster parents that he, to this day, refers to as Mom and Dad.

From the beginning of Tim's adult life, he was told that living independently wasn't possible for him. He was told time and again that he was "too low functioning". Tim, without knowing it, was fighting a battle all too familiar to people with disabilities, the battle of presumed incompetence. In this way of thinking, the skills necessary to live independently can never be discovered, for the only way someone can truly learn independent living skills is to live independently.

Tim kept asking to move out of his group home. He made formal requests, encouraged by a job coach, to his service coordinator at the San Diego Regional Center. All requests were dismissed. He repeatedly asked his foster parents, and they would always reply, "You aren't capable."

Tim, driven by the desire to live a fully included life, finally got his chance. He was referred to Life Works for services and in September 2005, he opted to work through an Essential Lifestyle Plan. Tim wanted Life Works to get to know him well before moving out. He invited 32 people to his first ELP, including his foster parents and his service coordinator. He also invited his "friends" as he knew them and other various people who were important to him.

Not one person that Tim invited showed up to this

meeting. That's right... not one! Not his foster parents, nor his house manager, nor his foster brothers or even his service coordinator. At this moment, Tim had his first realization that his life as he knew it wasn't very good. The relationships that he had weren't meaningful enough to support him in arguably the most important event of his life. He had purchased food for 32 people, prepared the meeting area for all of them, and was very excited for the event. When nobody showed up, Tim never flinched. He had the meeting with his facilitator and mapped out his dreams of life in the community as an independent adult. He remained positive, as he always is, throughout the process and didn't let the lack of attendance get in the way of his mission.

Tim's first apartment was in central San Diego. He lived with a roommate, a budding local rock musician. It turned out that Tim was living in an area that wasn't very safe; he ended up being mugged in his neighborhood and robbed in his own apartment. Therefore, Tim and his roommate decided to move to another part of San Diego. He settled in a community called North Park and felt much more secure in his surroundings.

On April 13, 2006, Tim had a PATH. It was during this process that Tim decided he wanted a different job. He had worked at a Pizza Hut restaurant for thirteen years, and now wanted to work at Albertson's supermarket. Tim also laid out plans for traveling to Las Vegas, learning to ride a bike, going to Disneyland, and having friends over for BBQs. Do you have any doubt whether Tim accomplished all these dreams?

Living independently, Tim was meeting his neighbors and developing relationships with them. He was building community for himself. Tim has an infectious personality and he naturally grasped the concept of reciprocity in a relationship. This ability, which was discovered after being afforded the opportunity, was amazing to watch. In the same year, Tim celebrated his 36th birthday party, and about 25 people attended. Since he was living in an environment that supported the idea of making sustainable relationships, people showed up. This was a stark contrast to that initial ELP.

Tim's reason for wanting to leave Pizza Hut was simple. He worked in the back of the restaurant, away from people, and because of that felt isolated and longed for connection with others. He felt that Albertson's supermarket would provide what he wanted, so he got a job there and soon became their "best employee" – words spoken by several of his fellow employees and managers. Tim had a natural work ethic; he was efficient, polite, learned quickly and was easy to get along with. He was, quite frankly, an employer's dream!

Life went on for Tim, working and living in San Diego. He was living a self-determined life, but something was missing. At all of his futures planning meetings, the resounding lament was that Tim wanted a girlfriend. He desired love.

In November 2007, he went on a blind date with a woman, Jamie, who also received supports from Life Works. Separately, Beth and Kirk each brought Tim and Jamie to the San Diego Zoo, a place both of them loved to visit. With every intention of needing to facilitate the date and conversations, we were astonished to find that we were insignificant in their world, which is what the zoo became that day... their world.

It was, in the purest form, love at first sight. They talked for hours, held hands and simply existed with each other as if they had known each other for years. Tim and Jamie began a long-distance relationship, as Jamie lived in San Marcos, a city about forty minutes north of San Diego. With the help of each other's support teams, Tim and Jamie spent weekend days together for over a year and a half.

Tim finally decided that he needed to be closer to Jamie. He talked to his circle of support team about the idea of moving to San Marcos to be closer to "his woman". He checked with Albertson's to see if he could transfer to one of their stores in San Marcos. Unfortunately, Albertson's did not have any positions available. What do you think Tim did?

He quit his job in the name of love and moved anyway! He took a risk, one afforded him because he lived a life where having the dignity of risk was a natural part of adult life.

Tim was confident that he would find a job because of his work history and references, and made the move to San Marcos in June 2009. With the help of an employment agency, Tim found a job at Camp Pendleton, a local Marine Corps Base in San Diego County. He works in one of the mess halls, where he has contact with hundreds of marines daily. It's a job where a good work ethic is recognized and praised, while offering Tim that human connection that is so important to him.

So, Tim met and fell in love with Jamie. He quit his job in San Diego, moved to San Marcos, got a great job and lived in his own apartment about two miles from Jamie's apartment. What could possibly be better? For Tim, it wasn't enough. The whole reason he identified wanting a girlfriend in all of his planning meetings was so he could eventually be married. Naturally, Tim wanted to take his relationship with Jamie to the next level.

With the help of one of his support team members and Jamie's mom, he looked at engagement rings that he thought she might like and planned his proposal. On the second anniversary of their meeting at the zoo, Tim planned a surprise proposal there, the site of their first date. Tim arranged with Jamie's support team that they take her on a trip to the zoo that day, and she didn't know that he was going to be there. He invited a handful of people to be in

On bended knee

attendance and arranged a dozen long-stemmed roses in a circle around him in a nook near where they met. Tim knew this was the perfect location, and as Jamie rounded the corner with some discreet choreography by each of their support workers, she found Tim encircled by roses, on one knee and ring in hand.

The crowd had grown to a good size as random passers-by stopped to watch this romantic occasion. It was a beautiful, powerful moment, one between two people madly in love with each other. She said yes, by the way!

In February 2010, Tim and Jamie decided to have a PATH done specifically to plan for their wedding, which was set for November 2010, around their third dating anniversary. At their PATH, Tim and Jamie identified their dream wedding. Tim is a Star Wars fanatic. Jamie is a huge fan of anything cheetah-related. She is even a member of a social group called the Cheetah Girls. They compromised with each other on what they each felt was important to have on their big day and decided that their honeymoon would be at the Disneyland Resort, where they would spend a couple of nights.

The ultimate fantasy of their PATH was the wish to travel to their honeymoon in true fairytale style. They wanted to leave the wedding site in a stretch Hummer limousine while the guests of the wedding blew bubbles and waved. They knew that weddings were expensive, and that saving for it themselves would be difficult. They also knew that prioritizing their wishes was critical when setting up their budget, which was created as a part of the PATH action plan.

In November 2010, Tim and Jamie were happily married at the Old Richardson School House, a popular and beautiful wedding spot in San Marcos. Tim stood proudly in his tuxedo, accompanied by his elegantly dressed groomsmen. Jamie's bridal party was nine women strong, all adorned in candy apple red formal dresses, matching the vests and ties of the groomsmen. Jamie and Tim exchanged vows that they wrote themselves. Jamie promised to love Tim through sickness and in health, while Tim promised to take care of his 'Dream Lover' forever. They exchanged rings and walked the aisle as husband and wife to the beautiful singing of Jamie's longtime friend, Jacquie Thousand.

Everything was perfect on this beautiful fall day. Upon being introduced at the reception by the DJ, Tim and Jamie triumphantly walked into the gathering under crossed light sabers à la Star Wars, held by their respective wedding parties. Tim and Jamie danced, ate, danced, laughed, danced, cried and danced some more.

At 8 p.m., a pearl-white stretch Hummer limousine drove slowly up the schoolhouse driveway. Tim and Jamie, freshly changed into traveling clothes and wearing matching Mickey and Minnie ear hats adorned with a veil and bowtie, walked through a crowd of cheering wedding guests who were blowing bubbles and hopped into their limousine.

The newlyweds

The smiles on their faces represented dreams achieved. The smiles and tears on the faces of their wedding guests represented the realization that living a fully inclusive life of one's dreams isn't a disability issue. People in attendance that day had a glimpse into the potential for a world that sees all people as equal. We saw Tim and Jamie, people once deemed not capable of living on their own in the community, live out their dream wedding, a wedding they planned and saved for in its entirety.

Saying goodbye before getting into the stretch limo

Tim and Jamie now live their customized life together. They are still happily married and saving for a house, as they planned out during a PATH. Tim recently received the Bravo Zulu Award on behalf of the mess hall team he works with at Camp Pendleton. The award was given for "excellence in effort and attitude". He is slowly working his way "off the grid" of services and state programs and he makes so much money at his job that he no longer receives an SSI benefit. He also no longer qualifies for the California Medical Assistance Program as he is carrying his medical insurance through his job and Blue Cross Medi-Care.

When he moved out of the group home with the help of Life Works, Tim received 24-hour supports. Tim, a man deemed incapable of living in the community independently, now receives support only a few days a week for a few hours at a time. He intended on having a good life and built a network of natural supports, and now has a community that has become his Intentional Team.

Tim accepting the Bravo Zulu Award

Tim and team member Teavy at his 40th birthday party

**We hope you will join us on the
Intentional Teaming Journey**

Beth & Kirk

- **Facilitation for Inclusion with PATH & MAPS** - training DVD
- **Conversations on Citizenship & Person-Centered Planning** - New
- **Who's Drawing the Lines? -** Judith Snow - new
- **Intentional Teaming -** Beth Gallagher & Kirk Hinkleman - new
- **Facilitating an Everyday Life -** J. Lord, C. Dingwall, B. Leavitt - new
- **Equity, Social Justice and Disability in Schools -** Gary Bunch et al - new
- PATH & MAPS Handbook: Person-Centered Ways to Build Community (NEW)
- Gentle Heart Fearless Mind: Mindfulness DVD + Booklet: Alan Sloan
- Friends & Inclusion: Five Approaches to Building Relationships: P. Hutchison; J. Lord, K. Lord (NEW)
- Make a Difference Pack: Leader's Manual + MAD Guidebook +10 Learning Journey Booklets
- Golden Reflections: - written by Vargus Yale (Mike's seeing-eye guide dog) with Mike Yale
     Also available in Audio MP3 read by Don Harron and as a package with the book
- Inclusive Education: Emergent Solutions   Gary Bunch & Angela Valeo
- Planning for a Real Life After School: Transition from School (2 editions)
- The Poetry of David Moreau: If You're Happy and You Know It Clap Your Hand
- Doing Our Best Work: 10 Ingredients of Quality Support: Peter Leidy - DVD
- ABCD in Action - DVD & Book -When People Care Enough to Act
- My Life My Choice - DVD - Seven Adults living full lives in the community
- Make a Difference - book; Leaders Guide, Work Booklets
- The Big Plan - A Good Life After School - Transition Planning with groups
- Each Belongs - book & CD - The 1st Inclusive School Board ever!
- PlayFair Teams - 2 books, DVD + Posters - blended teams in schools.
- Find Meaning in the Work - CD & Manual/Curriculum - presentation ready!

INCLUSION PRESS

47 Indian Trail, Toronto,

Ontario Canada M6R 1Z8

p. 416.658.5363   f. 416.658.5067

e. inclusionpress@inclusion.com

inclusion.com   BOOKS • WORKSHOPS • MEDIA • RESOURCES